DISCOVER WHAT'S INSIDE

LET'S GET STARTED

Lethal lions, venomous snakes, powerful orcas ... what do all of these creatures have in common? They're PREDATORS. A predator is an animal that hunts and kills other animals for food. If a creature is at the top of the food chain in the area in which it lives, we call it an "**apex** predator".

In this book, you will find animal predators of all kinds, with points assigned for their deadliness in the following categories:

- their deadly details

- their killer weapons

- how they attack their prey or a predator.

These points will be added up to give the animal's overall predator score.

Abbreviation chart:

oz = ounces	in = inches	mph = miles per hour
lbs = pounds	ft = feet	

SCARY STATS

This category will account for the animal's size, speed, strength or success rate – basically, any numbers or rankings that set this animal apart as an effective or terrifying hunter. Remember, it's not always the biggest animals that can cause the most damage among prey populations.

SCARY STATS: 6/10
TERRIFYING TECHNIQUES: 5/10
LETHAL WEAPONS: 6/10
PREDATOR SCORE: 17/30

TERRIFYING TECHNIQUES

All predators have developed their own individual methods of hunting, catching and killing their prey – depending on the situation and what they're hoping to eat. This category will give points according to the skill, ingenuity, intelligence or sheer gruesomeness of the animal's techniques.

LETHAL WEAPONS

Talons, fangs, muscles, venom: nature has armed creatures with a frightening array of weapons – and that's not even including eyesight, hearing or other senses that can mean there really is nowhere for prey animals to hide.

PREDATOR SCORE

All the points added up make for the overall predator score. Now let's meet 50 creatures who you might just find haunting your nightmares!

MURDEROUS MAMMALS

Claws, teeth and intelligence – the predators in this category have it all. Mammals are vertebrate animals that are warm-blooded and feed their young with milk. Lots of the predators in this list belong to the *felid* (cat) or *canid* (dog) families but there are also bears and even marsupials that are predators!

FOSSA

(Scientific name: Cryptoprocta ferox)

Eats: small to medium-sized animals – mostly lemurs but also rodents, reptiles, birds, insects and crabs

The largest predator native to Madagascar, the fossa has a completely meat-based diet, and is the number one predator of lemurs. During the breeding season, fossae hunt in groups.

SCARY STATS:

Measuring 70–80 centimetres (27.5–31 in) with tails 65–70 centimetres (25.6–27.5 in) and weighing around 5.5 to 8.6 kilograms (12.1 to 18.9 lbs), fossae are on the smaller side for our predatory mammals. But they are still large relative to other predators in Madagascar, and they use this advantage to deadly effect.

TERRIFYING TECHNIQUES:

Fossae hunt either on the ground or in trees. When hunting in groups, one fossa will chase the prey through the branches and down to the ground where others are waiting to overpower it. Fossae are known to rip out the innards of their larger lemur prey.

LETHAL WEAPONS:

Fossae use their semi-retractable claws, long tails, flexible ankles and the padded soles of their paws to hunt prey through trees. Like many nocturnal predators, they have eyes that reflect light. They also have sharp cat-like teeth to use on their prey once they've captured them.

PREDATOR POINTS

SCARY STATS: 5/10

TERRIFYING TECHNIQUES: 6/10

LETHAL WEAPONS: 5/10

PREDATOR SCORE: 16/30

WELL-ADAPTED PREDATORS TO BE FEARED – ESPECIALLY IF YOU'RE A LEMUR!

9

TASMANIAN DEVIL

(Scientific name: *Sarcophilus harrisii*)

Eats: wombats, sheep, fish, birds, insects, frogs, reptiles and even small kangaroos

Famous for their noisy eating habits, Tasmanian devils can deliver one of the strongest bites of any land mammal, and have even been known to chew through metal!

PREDATOR POINTS

SCARY STATS: 5/10

TERRIFYING TECHNIQUES: 5/10

LETHAL WEAPONS: 7/10

PREDATOR SCORE: 17/30

FEROCIOUS MARSUPIALS WITH HORRIBLE TABLE MANNERS!

SCARY STATS:

Tasmanian devils are not heavyweights amongst predatory mammals. Males tend to be larger than females, measuring an average 65 centimetres (25.6 in) head to body, with tails of around 26 centimetres (10.2 in) and typically weighing around 8 kilograms (17.6 lbs). They can reach speeds of 13 kilometres per hour (8 mph), though only for short distances.

TERRIFYING TECHNIQUES:

Tasmanian devils are opportunistic predators and eat dead animal carcasses more often than they hunt live prey. When they are hunting, they don't tend to work together – it's every devil for himself or herself! In fact, fierce fights often break out over food. Tasmanian devils eat every part of the animal – nothing is wasted!

LETHAL WEAPONS:

Tasmanian devils' number one weapon is their incredibly powerful jaws which they can open to 75–80 degrees. However, they also have long claws that allow them to grip their victims strongly as well as sharp teeth, and whiskers that help them to find prey in the dark.

SCARY STATS: 6/10

TERRIFYING TECHNIQUES: 6/10

LETHAL WEAPONS: 6/10

PREDATOR SCORE: 18/30

THE PERFECT HUNTING ANIMAL
SINCE ANCIENT TIMES

CARACAL WILD CAT

(Scientific name: Caracal caracal)

Eats: small mammals, birds and rodents

8

These unusual-looking medium-sized cats have been used by humans for hunting since ancient times. Despite this, the highly secretive creatures have proved hard to observe in the wild.

SCARY STATS:

These wild cats weigh 8–18 kilograms (17.6–39.6 lbs). They can leap up to 3 metres (9.8 ft) in the air, and take down prey two to three times their own size.

TERRIFYING TECHNIQUES:

These wild cats are skilful hunters. They stealthily stalk their prey and can even snatch it from the air. Once the prey is captured, they kill it with a bite to the throat or the back of the neck.

LETHAL WEAPONS:

These cats have strong lower jaws and long canine teeth, which help them deliver the death bite. They also have sharp retractable claws and powerful hind legs.

KILLER FACT

PEOPLE USED TO PLACE BETS ON HOW MANY BIRDS A WILD CAT COULD TAKE DOWN WITH ONE SWIPE! THIS MAY BE THE ORIGIN OF THE PHRASE "TO PUT THE CAT AMONG THE PIGEONS".

PREDATOR POINTS

SCARY STATS: 5/10

TERRIFYING TECHNIQUES: 5/10

LETHAL WEAPONS: 9/10

PREDATOR SCORE: 19/30

FEROCIOUS AND RESOURCEFUL –
A NATURAL KILLER

HONEY BADGER

(Scientific name: Mellivora capensis)

Eats: insects, rodents, birds, frogs, snakes, tortoises,
turtles, lizards, eggs (and honey!)

These intelligent animals are well known for their ferocity and strength. They get their name from their love of honey – they'll fearlessly attack beehives to get at it!

SCARY STATS:

At lengths of 55–77 centimetres (21.6–30.3 in), and weights of 9–16 kilograms (19.8–35.3 lbs), it is not size that makes honey badgers so fearsome.

TERRIFYING TECHNIQUES:

Honey badgers will dig to reach insect or rodent prey and have no fear of bee stings. They have also been known to tear bark off trees or lift stones to get at prey.

KILLER FACT

HONEY BADGERS ARE ALMOST TIRELESS FIGHTERS.

LETHAL WEAPONS:

Forceful jaws allow honey badgers to feed on tortoises. They also have very strong claws and skin so tough that they have few predators themselves. In addition to their natural weapons, they are also one of very few species capable of using tools such as sticks and rocks to catch or kill prey.

SNOW LEOPARD

(Scientific name: *Panthera uncia*)

Eats: mammals of all sizes (but the bigger the better!)

These well-camouflaged felines are the least aggressive to humans of all big cats. But that doesn't mean they're not deadly when hunting.

LETHAL WEAPONS:

Excellent natural camouflage assists snow leopards with their surprise attacks. Their broad paws allow them to walk on snow, and as they are covered in fur, the sound of their approach is muffled. Their short, powerful forelimbs and strong chest muscles are ideal for climbing and making brief sprints through rugged terrain.

PREDATOR POINTS

SCARY STATS: 7/10

TERRIFYING TECHNIQUES: 7/10

LETHAL WEAPONS: 6/10

PREDATOR SCORE: 20/30

SHY CREATURES BUT PERFECTLY ADAPTED TO TERRIFY THEIR PREY

SCARY STATS:

With head-to-body lengths of 75–150 centimetres (27.5–59 in), tails of 80–105 centimetres (31.5–41.3 in) and an average weight of 22–55 kilograms (48.5–121.2 lbs), snow leopards can use their bulk, combined with their hunting tactics, to take down and kill animals over twice their own size.

TERRIFYING TECHNIQUES:

Snow leopards prefer to hide and then ambush their victims from above. They will use the momentum of their initial jump to pursue prey for up to 300 metres (984.2 ft), and then kill it with a bite to the neck. They consume all edible parts of an animal.

GREY WOLF

(Scientific name: Canis lupus)

Eats: large and medium-sized mammals

5

Feared by humans throughout history, wolves hunt in packs and travel constantly in search of prey. From their spine-tingling howls to their super-sharp teeth, wolves are fierce killer creatures.

SCARY STATS:

Male wolves tend to be larger than females, averaging 44 kilograms (97 lbs), and 105–160 centimetres (41.3–63 in) head to body. Wolves can run at 55–70 kilometres per hour (34.2–43.5 mph) and can maintain this for at least 20 minutes. One leap can take them 5 metres (16.4 ft) into the air.

TERRIFYING TECHNIQUES:

Wolves use smell and hearing to locate their victims, and hunt by stalking. They employ different techniques depending on the prey. For bigger groups, they attack the rear and sides, or try to isolate a lone victim. Wolves also have different methods depending on the size of the prey – they go for the throat of medium-sized animals, but generally leap and pin down smaller victims.

LETHAL WEAPONS:

Wolves have long legs, allowing them to move swiftly through snow, as well as strong jaws and large, heavy teeth, suitable for crushing bone. They have a sharp sense of hearing, which they use to find their prey. Though they also use their sense of smell, it is not as strong as in other hunting dog species.

PREDATOR POINTS

SCARY STATS: 7/10

TERRIFYING TECHNIQUES: 8/10

LETHAL WEAPONS: 6/10

PREDATOR SCORE: 21/30

PREY BEWARE WHEN YOU HEAR A WOLF'S HOWL!

10

SCARY STATS: 7/10

TERRIFYING TECHNIQUES: 9/10

LETHAL WEAPONS: 7/10

PREDATOR SCORE: 23/30

THESE ENDANGERED WILD DOGS
ARE THE PERFECT PREDATOR

AFRICAN WILD DOGS

(Scientific name: Lycaon pictus)

Eats: mammals especially antelope, but also impala, springbok, wildebeest, warthog, ostrich and more

These hyper-carnivorous animals are highly successful hunters, partly due to the fact that they can alter their techniques depending on the prey.

4

SCARY STATS:

Smaller than their *canid* wolf cousins, African wild dogs tend to weigh 20–25 kilograms (44–55.1 lbs), and measure 75–109 centimetres (29.5–42.9 in). What they lack in size they make up in speed and stamina, as they are able to run at up to 66 kilometres per hour (41 mph) for as long as an hour. Their hunting success rates are 60% and higher!

TERRIFYING TECHNIQUES:

These clever predators vary their hunting strategies depending on the prey. They hunt in large, coordinated packs. Bigger prey is repeatedly bitten on the hindquarters until forced to stop; wildebeests are rushed at in order to panic the herd and separate individuals; antelope are chased until exhausted and caught by cutting off their escape routes.

LETHAL WEAPONS:

Sharp teeth and a powerful bite help to tear meat and break bone, increasing the speed at which prey can be consumed – African wild dogs can eat 1.2–5.9 kilograms (2.6–13 lbs) per day. They also have long legs, important in maintaining their running speed.

SCARY STATS: 8/10

TERRIFYING TECHNIQUES: 8/10

LETHAL WEAPONS: 8/10

PREDATOR SCORE: 24/30

MIGHTY AND FEARSOME ARCTIC HUNTERS

POLAR BEAR

(Scientific name: *Ursus maritimus*)

Eats: mostly seals but also reindeer, muskox, birds, eggs, rodents, crabs and other crustaceans

These huge specialized seal-hunters are the most carnivorous members of the bear family and the apex predator in their chilly natural habitat.

3

SCARY STATS:

At 350–700 kilograms (771.6–1543.2 lbs), and standing up to 2 metres (6.6 ft) tall, polar bears are massive! Their top sprinting speed is 40 kilometres per hour (24.8 mph).

TERRIFYING TECHNIQUES:

When hunting seals, the bears lie in wait by their breathing holes in the ice, and use their forepaws to drag prey out, before crushing its skull using their teeth.

KILLER FACT

POLAR BEAR ATTACKS ARE ALMOST ALWAYS FATAL FOR THE VICTIM.

LETHAL WEAPONS:

Polar bears' sharp teeth are very important for their meat-based diet. Their highly developed sense of smell allows them to sniff out seals from 1.6 kilometres (1 mile) away and 1 metre (3.3 ft) under ice, and their giant feet are perfect for walking or running on snow, and for propelling them through the water.

LION

(Scientific name: Panthera leo)

Eats: mammals, especially wildebeest, zebra, buffalo, giraffe, deer and wild boar

Apex predators in their habitat, lions become effective hunters before they are two years old. These ROAR-some predators are a force to be reckoned with.

LETHAL WEAPONS:

Lions are muscular animals, with strong necks, legs and claws that, combined with the pride's teamwork, allow them to hunt, immobilize and kill the largest prey of any land mammal. They also have huge teeth, and sometimes use their jaws to cover an animal's mouth and nose, killing it by suffocation.

TERRIFYING TECHNIQUES:

Prides coordinate their hunts, with each member performing a different role or taking up a different position. So smaller weaker lionesses will surround the prey and larger ones will bring it down. Lions will only run in short bursts. They take advantage of factors that limit visibility, such as darkness, and kill prey by strangulation.

SCARY STATS:

Lions are the second-largest cat species. Lionesses (who do the hunting for a pride of lions) measure 1.4–1.7 metres (4.5–5.7 ft) and weigh 120–182 kilograms (264.5–401.2 lbs). They can take down prey twice their own size, and require 5–7 kilograms (11–15.4 lbs) of meat per day. They can reach speeds of 81 kilometres per hour (50.3 mph).

PREDATOR POINTS

SCARY STATS: 9/10
TERRIFYING TECHNIQUES: 9/10
LETHAL WEAPONS: 8/10
PREDATOR SCORE: 26/30

THE RULERS OF THE SAVANNAH

TIGER

(Scientific name: Panthera tigris)

Eats: small and medium-sized mammals

The largest of all cat species, tigers are such ferocious hunters that they even prey on other predators!

Did you know?

Domestic cats might not like water but tigers are strong swimmers!

SCARY STATS:

Tigers can reach speeds of 49–65 kilometres per hour (30.4–40.4 mph), although only in short bursts. Tiger hunt success rates range from 5–50%. The Bengal tiger is the biggest subspecies, measuring 270–310 centimetres (106.2–122 in) and weighing 180–258 kilograms (396.8–568.7 lbs). Their roars can be heard from 3 kilometres (1.86 miles) away!

LETHAL WEAPONS:

Tigers use their massive size and strength to knock prey off balance, hold it down and even drag it away once dead. Their paws are powerful enough to smash skulls and break backs, and their famous stripes are useful for camouflage so that they can stay hidden before pouncing.

TERRIFYING TECHNIQUES:

These apex predators prefer bigger prey, which they kill by biting the throat while keeping it pinned down. When killing smaller animals they break the neck or pierce the windpipe. They may also swipe with their paws. They use ambush techniques to attack from any angle. Cubs are taught to hunt when they are just a few months old.

PREDATOR POINTS

SCARY STATS: 10/10

TERRIFYING TECHNIQUES: 9/10

LETHAL WEAPONS: 9/10

PREDATOR SCORE: 28/30

SOLITARY BUT LETHAL HUNTERS

CROSSWORD

**Read the previous chapter, then use the clues
to complete the crossword!**

CLUES

Across

1. Honey badgers are well known for their ferocity and _____.

2. This is a Tasmanian devil's number one weapon.

3. A tiger's stripes are useful for this.

4. African wild dogs hunt these down until they're exhausted.

Down

1. A polar bear mostly eats these.

5. The sharpest sense of a grey wolf is their _____.

6. This mammal becomes an effective hunter before it is
   two years old.

7. This mammal causes more human deaths by direct attack than
   any other wild animal.

Answers on page 74

SAVAGE SEA LIFE

The predators of the sea come in many different shapes and sizes. They are mammals, fish, squid, jellyfish and even sea anemones. They have different prey and different techniques for killing them. The one thing these sea creatures all have in common is how deadly they are.

COMB JELLIES

(Scientific name: Ctenophore)

Eats: animal plankton and other microscopic organisms; some eat crustaceans, molluscs, fish larvae and jellyfish

The rainbow effect of their cones may give these jellies a pretty and dreamlike appearance – but they are also lethal predators of the sea.

SCARY STATS:

Comb jellies size varies depending on species, but they tend to be small predators, reaching a maximum length of 15 centimetres (5.9 in). However they can eat up to ten times their own body weight in a day. Comb jellies are perfectly adapted to move through the seas, being 95% water themselves!

TERRIFYING TECHNIQUES:

These predators employ a range of different techniques for capturing their prey, including netting it in their tentacles, using their large mouths to engulf it whole before clamping shut, and generating a current to waft the prey into their mouths. Once caught, the prey is turned into liquid and digested by their cells.

LETHAL WEAPONS:

The "combs" in this jellies' name are eight rows of microscopic hairs that run up and down their bodies and propel them through the water – they are the largest animals known to have this feature. Many comb jellies also have tentacles with sticky cells, which they use like fishing rods to catch prey.

PREDATOR POINTS

SCARY STATS: 4/10
TERRIFYING TECHNIQUES: 6/10
LETHAL WEAPONS: 6/10
PREDATOR SCORE: 16/30
PRETTY BUT LETHAL

PREDATOR POINTS

SCARY STATS: 5/10

TERRIFYING TECHNIQUES: 6/10

LETHAL WEAPONS: 7/10

PREDATOR SCORE: 18/30

QUICK, STRONG AND VICIOUS

GREAT BARRACUDA

(Scientific name: Sphyraena barracuda)

Eats: a wide range of fish including snapper, small tuna, herring, anchovy and mullet

9

These hungry ambush predators can deliver a savage bite, and have been known to follow divers and swimmers if they mistake them for prey.

SCARY STATS:

Most are 60–100 centimetres (23.6–39.3 in); but especially large ones can reach 1.5 metres (4.9 ft). They typically weigh 2.5–9 kilograms (5.5–19.8 lbs) and can hit speeds of 43 kilometres per hour (26.7 mph) for short spurts.

TERRIFYING TECHNIQUES:

Great barracudas rely on the element of surprise as well as speed to overtake their prey. They are able to bite large fish in half!

KILLER FACT

THE HEAVIEST-KNOWN WEIGHT OF ANY GREAT BARRACUDA IS 45 KILOGRAMS (99.2 LBS).

LETHAL WEAPONS:

Keen senses of sight and smell allow these predators to locate their victims. They have strong jaws and two rows of knife-sharp teeth, which they use to deadly effect. These teeth also lock shut, preventing smaller prey from escaping once swallowed. Great barracudas' streamlined bodies are perfectly designed for speed.

SEA ANEMONE

(Scientific name: Actiniaria)

Eats: fish, mussels, plankton and worms

Another sea creature whose beautiful appearance hides a range of terrifying weapons and techniques that make it an effective predator is the common sea anemone.

LETHAL WEAPONS:

Sea anemone tentacles can be extended and are armed with stinging cells. A touch to these tentacles triggers tiny harpoon-like weapons to explode and inject prey or attackers with venom, which paralyses them so they can then be easily brought to the sea anemone's mouth.

PREDATOR POINTS

SCARY STATS: 3/10

TERRIFYING TECHNIQUES: 7/10

LETHAL WEAPONS: 9/10

PREDATOR SCORE: 19/30

BEAUTIFUL BUT WELL-ARMED

SCARY STATS:

Most sea anemones are very small, measuring 1–5 centimetres (0.39–1.96 in) across and 1.5–10 centimetres (0.39–3.93 in) in length, though they are inflatable. The largest examples are as big as 1 metre (3.28 ft). There are as many as 1000 different species of sea anemone around the world.

TERRIFYING TECHNIQUES:

Sea anemones mostly stay in the same position. When they do move, it is so slowly that it cannot be seen by the naked eye. They can use their tentacles and stinging cells to subdue prey and to guide it into their mouths. They can also open their mouths to swallow larger prey whole.

SWORDFISH

(Scientific name: Xiphias gladius)

Eats: a wide range of fish including mackerel, herring, silver hake, squid and crustaceans

Though the sword that gives them their name is not used to spear prey, as you might expect, these fish are nonetheless skilful predators of the sea.

PREDATOR POINTS

SCARY STATS: 7/10

TERRIFYING TECHNIQUES: 6/10

LETHAL WEAPONS: 7/10

PREDATOR SCORE: 20/30

FAST AND CAPABLE OF DELIVERING A CRUEL CUT

SCARY STATS:

These big fish commonly reach 3 metres (9.84 ft) – the maximum recorded size is 4.55 metres (14.9 ft) – and weigh up to a massive 650 kilograms (1433 lbs). Despite their considerable bulk, they are among the fastest fish. They can reach top speeds of over 90 kilometres per hour (56 mph)!

TERRIFYING TECHNIQUES:

Swordfish depend on their impressive speed and agility in the water to overcome prey. Their "sword" is not used to spear fish, as we might predict, but rather to slash at and injure larger ones, so that they can be more easily captured. Smaller prey is swallowed whole.

LETHAL WEAPONS:

Swordfish are well evolved for speed – and quick recovery afterwards – with powerful tails, and big hearts and gills. In addition to their speed and their swords, swordfish also have special organs next to their eyes which heat the eyes and brain, helping them to spot quick-moving prey.

SCARY STATS: 4/10

TERRIFYING TECHNIQUES: 8/10

LETHAL WEAPONS: 9/10

PREDATOR SCORE: 21/30

PERFECTLY DESIGNED HUNTING MACHINES

LIONFISH

(Scientific name: Pterois)

Eats: small fish, invertebrates and molluscs

These skilled hunters are armed with a whole range of tools to help them capture and kill their prey.

6

SCARY STATS:

Lionfish's deadly powers don't lie in their size: they average 33–40 centimetres (13–16 in) and weigh between 25 grams (0.05 lbs) and 1.5 kilograms (3.3 lbs).

TERRIFYING TECHNIQUES:

Lionfish can blow jets of water to disorient and steer prey, and then spread their fins to swallow it in one go.

LETHAL WEAPONS:

These fish have specialized muscles, which allow them to change their centre of gravity to attract prey. Their fin rays are also powerfully venomous.

KILLER FACT

YOUNG LIONFISH HAVE A TENTACLE ABOVE THEIR EYE SOCKETS TO ATTRACT PREY.

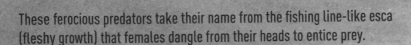

5

ANGLERFISH

(Scientific name: Lophiiformes)

Eats: a wide range of fish of all sizes

These ferocious predators take their name from the fishing line-like esca (fleshy growth) that females dangle from their heads to entice prey.

SCARY STATS:

Anglerfish vary in size, ranging from 20 centimetres (7.8 in) to over 1 metre (3.2 ft) long, and weighing up to 45 kilograms (99 lbs). Their jaws and stomachs can expand to accommodate prey twice their own size. They can dart forwards but mostly drift, moving at around 0.24 body lengths per second.

TERRIFYING TECHNIQUES:

Females dangle their lure to attract prey, then rush forwards to seize it. Some can open their mouths to several times their original size in a fraction of a second and create a suction effect to drag their victims in. They have been observed floating upside down with their escas dangling – a low-effort method of hunting!

LETHAL WEAPONS:

As well as their personal, sometimes luminous fishing-rod escas, anglerfish have enormous mouths (that in most subspecies go the whole way round the head) full of dagger-sharp teeth, which are angled inwards, the better for grabbing prey. The teeth can also be lowered to allow victims to travel smoothly to the stomach.

PREDATOR POINTS

SCARY STATS: 4/10

TERRIFYING TECHNIQUES: 9/10

LETHAL WEAPONS: 9/10

PREDATOR SCORE: 22/30

NATURE'S FEARSOME FISHERMEN

HAMMERHEAD SHARK

(Scientific name: Sphyrnidae)

Eats: fish (including other sharks), squid, octopus and crustaceans

4

The name of these distinctive-looking sharks needs no explanation. Though they might look funny their methods of hunting are anything but.

SCARY STATS:

Again, these sharks vary a lot in size, measuring 0.9–6 metres (3–19.7 ft) and weighing 3–580 kilograms (6.6–1279 lbs). Their mouths are disproportionately small compared to their large heads. The position of their eyes allows for 360-degree vision.

TERRIFYING TECHNIQUES:

Hammerhead sharks use their famous heads to stun and pin down prey, before eating it. They often stalk their victims at the bottom of the ocean, but they have also been known to attack humans unprovoked, and to eat other hammerheads. They usually hunt alone and at night.

LETHAL WEAPONS:

In addition to their weapon-like heads, the structure of these sharks' spines also allows for maximum manoeuvrability and sharp-turning, making them agile hunters. The pores (tiny holes) in a shark's skin can detect the electricity given off by other creatures – yet another helpful tool when hunting.

PREDATOR POINTS

SCARY STATS: 8/10

TERRIFYING TECHNIQUES: 9/10

LETHAL WEAPONS: 7/10

PREDATOR SCORE: 24/30

HUGE AND AGGRESSIVE HUNTERS

LEOPARD SEAL

(Scientific name: Hydruga leptonyx)

Eats: krill, squid, fish, penguins and even young elephant seals

Second only to the killer whale among Antarctica's predators, these hunters are the scourge of penguins, but can also be dangerous to humans.

SCARY STATS:

Measuring 2.4–3.5 metres (7.8–11.6ft) and weighing 200–600 kilograms (441–1323 lbs), leopard seals are not creatures you would like to encounter when in the water!

TERRIFYING TECHNIQUES:

These vicious killers grab penguins by the feet, shaking them violently and bashing their bodies against the water to kill them. When penguin isn't on the menu, they sieve krill from the water using their teeth.

KILLER FACT

LEOPARD SEALS HAVE BEEN OBSERVED HUNTING PENGUINS AND OTHER PREY FOR FUN – EVEN WHEN THEY'RE NOT HUNGRY!

LETHAL WEAPONS:

Leopard seals' main weapons are their strength and massive bulk. Despite their long (2.5 centimetres; 0.9 in) canines, their teeth aren't well-suited to cutting prey into bitesize chunks, so they instead thrash it around to tear it into smaller pieces. Their streamlined bodies allow them to move through the water quickly.

ORCA

(Scientific name: Orcinus orca)

Eats: fish, mammals, sea birds and sea turtles

The number one predator of Antarctica, orcas employ a range of lethal hunting techniques from stunning victims with their powerful tails, to holding prey upside down in the water.

2

LETHAL WEAPONS:

These apex predators have sharp senses of hearing, sight and touch. They use the echoes of their own clicks to locate prey. Their brains are the second-heaviest among marine mammals and this is reflected in their intelligence. They have strong teeth and jaws.

TERRIFYING TECHNIQUES:

Orcas use different hunting tactics depending on the prey. They immobilize sharks and rays by holding them upside down. To catch herring, they force them into a ball formation, which they then smack with their tails. This technique can catch them up to 15 herring at a time. They often disable their prey first to prevent injury to themselves.

SCARY STATS:

These are gigantic creatures, with the largest of the species measuring a whopping 6–8 metres (19.7–26.2 ft) and weighing more than 6000 kilograms (6 tonnes). Their dorsal fins alone average 1.8 metres (5.9 ft). They eat around 227 kilograms (500 lbs) a day. Despite their size, orcas can swim at up to 54 kilometres per hour (33.5 mph).

PREDATOR POINTS

SCARY STATS: 10/10

TERRIFYING TECHNIQUES: 9/10

LETHAL WEAPONS: 9/10

PREDATOR SCORE: 28/30

SOPHISTICATED AND SKILFUL HUNTERS

COLOSSAL SQUID

(Scientific name: *Mesonychoteuthis hamiltoni*)

Eats: large fish such as toothfish and other squid

Living at a depth of about 2.2 kilometres (1.37 miles), the colossal squid is perhaps the most mysterious predator of all. It has never even been captured on camera alive!

Did you know?
The largest recorded colossal squid was captured in 2007 by a New Zealand fishing boat.

SCARY STATS:

Most of what scientists know about the colossal squid comes from remains found in the stomachs of sperm whales. From this and other remnants gathered, it seems that the squid measures 12–14 metres (39.3–46 ft) and weighs up to a hefty 750 kilograms (1653.4 lbs). Their eyes – used for locating prey – are the largest of any creature's ever documented.

TERRIFYING TECHNIQUES:

Like so much else about this species, their methods of hunting have not been observed in the wild. However, it is thought that they are ambush predators that use bioluminescence to attract prey, locating them with their massive eyes, which are perfectly adapted to the dark at the depths at which they live.

LETHAL WEAPONS:

While the giant squid's arms and tentacles only have suckers lined with small teeth, the colossal squid's are also equipped with sharp hooks. Some of these swivel and some are three-pointed, making them truly terrifying weapons. Their beaks are also larger and more robust than those of any other squid.

PREDATOR POINTS

SCARY STATS: 10/10

TERRIFYING TECHNIQUES: 9/10

LETHAL WEAPONS: 10/10

PREDATOR SCORE: 29/30

MYSTERIOUS MONSTERS OF THE DEEP

KILLER FACT

COLOSSAL SQUIDS HAVE LIGHT ORGANS ON THEIR EYEBALLS THAT ACT AS HEADLIGHTS, ENABLING THEM TO SEE PREY IN THE DARK.

SPOT THE DIFFERENCE

Can you spot **EIGHT** differences between these pictures?

TRUE OR FALSE?

Can you say if the statements below are true or false?

	TRUE	FALSE
1. Comb jellies bodies are 10% water.		
2. Sea anemone tentacles are armed with stinging cells.		
3. Swordfish use their swords to spear fish.		
4. Lionfish can blow jets of water to steer their prey.		
5. Anglerfish can expand their stomach to eat prey twice their own size.		
6. Leopard seals do not like eating penguins.		
7. Orcas immobilize sharks by holding them upside down.		
8. Colossal squid cannot see in the dark.		

Answers on page 74

AGGRESSIVE AMPHIBIANS AND REPTILES

When it comes to amphibian and reptile predators, nature has come up with a whole range of methods and weapons. Whether it's toxic venom, hooked claws or long fangs you're facing, being the prey of any of these reptiles or amphibians would be no fun!

MEXICAN BEADED LIZARD

(Scientific name: Heloderma horridum)

Eats: mostly bird and reptile eggs; sometimes small birds, mammals, lizards, insects and frogs

These specialized nest predators mostly eat the eggs of other reptiles as well as birds.

SCARY STATS:

At 57–91 centimetres (22.4–91.8 in) and around 800 grams (1.76 lbs), these lizards are significantly larger than the famous gila monster to which they are related, but they don't rely on their size for their predatory success.

TERRIFYING TECHNIQUES:

Mexican beaded lizards are specialized nest predators, used to hunting through the treetops for eggs left unattended. They use their tongues to smell and seek prey, and can climb, burrow and swim. One of two venomous lizard species found in Mexico, they chew their victims to get venom-laced saliva into the wound.

LETHAL WEAPONS:

As well as being able to smell using their tongues, Mexican beaded lizards have strong jaw grips, allowing them to hang on to prey for long enough to get venom into them. However, their teeth are easily broken. Their venom can cause falling blood pressure and heart and lung failure.

PREDATOR POINTS

SCARY STATS: 4/10

TERRIFYING TECHNIQUES: 7/10

LETHAL WEAPONS: 5/10

PREDATOR SCORE: 16/30

DELIVERING A NASTY CHEW

SCARY STATS: 5/10

TERRIFYING TECHNIQUES: 6/10

LETHAL WEAPONS: 6/10

PREDATOR SCORE: 17/30

THE ULTIMATE LETHAL HUGGER

BOA CONSTRICTOR

(Scientific name: Boa constrictor)

Eats: small to medium-sized mammals and birds

These snake's famous method of killing prey has long been the stuff of legends . . . and nightmares.

SCARY STATS:

Females are usually larger than males and measure up to a terrifying 4 metres (13 ft). They weigh 10–15 kilograms (22–33 lbs).

TERRIFYING TECHNIQUES:

Normally, a boa will sit and wait to ambush its prey, but occasionally the deadly snake will head out to hunt. They grab prey with their teeth and then wrap themselves around it, squeezing it to death before swallowing it whole.

KILLER FACT

BOAS HAVE DISTINCTIVE PATTERNS, WHICH VARY DEPENDING ON THE HABITAT THEY LIVE IN AND MUST CAMOUFLAGE INTO.

LETHAL WEAPONS:

Boa constrictors have special cells in their lips which can sense heat, helping them to locate their prey. They use their hefty size to crush victims to death – scientists now believe this works by cutting off the vital blood flow rather than causing suffocation. They can also deliver a painful bite using their small, hooked teeth.

ASIAN WATER MONITOR

(Scientific name: Varanus salvator)

Eats: fish, frogs, rodents, birds, snakes and crabs

8

The world's second-heaviest lizard after the Komodo dragon, the Asian water monitor is a chunky and formidable hunter.

LETHAL WEAPONS:

These large creatures have muscular bodies, powerful legs which help them to climb and swim, and strong tails. They also have mighty jaws, sharp claws and many jagged teeth, all of which they use for defence as well as hunting. Their bites can cut tendons and veins.

TERRIFYING TECHNIQUES:

Water monitors have been observed holding prey with their front legs and tearing chunks off it with their teeth. They are excellent at both swimming and climbing. It is thought by some scientists that they may have venom which they use in capturing and killing prey.

SCARY STATS:

Measuring 1.5–2 metres (4.9–6.6 ft) and weighing 3.5–7.6 kilograms (7.7–16.7 lbs), these are massive creatures. Some mega-monitors can grow to 3 metres (9.8 ft) long! They can stay underwater for up to 30 minutes while hunting for prey.

PREDATOR POINTS

SCARY STATS: 6/10

TERRIFYING TECHNIQUES: 6/10

LETHAL WEAPONS: 6/10

PREDATOR SCORE: 18/30

MUSCLY CREATURES WITH TERRIFYING TEETH AND CLAWS

TREE CROCODILE

(Scientific name: Varanus salvadorii)

Eats: birds, bats, rodents, eggs and small mammals

Another species of monitor, tree crocodiles are the top predator in New Guinea.

SCARY STATS:

One of the longest species of lizard in the world, tree crocodiles typically grow up to 2.4 metres (7.8 ft), but there are claims of much bigger individuals. They weigh up to 90 kilograms (200 lbs).

TERRIFYING TECHNIQUES:

These lizards are known for being aggressive and unpredictable. They are able to anticipate where prey will run, which allows them to meet it head-on.

PREDATOR POINTS

SCARY STATS: 7/10

TERRIFYING TECHNIQUES: 6/10

LETHAL WEAPONS: 6/10

PREDATOR SCORE: 19/30

SPEEDY AND BAD-TEMPERED

KILLER FACT

THESE LIZARDS' TAILS ARE LONGER THAN THEIR BODIES – THEY'RE USEFUL FOR BALANCE AND DEFENCE.

LETHAL WEAPONS:

Tree crocodiles' teeth are well-adapted for seizing the fast-moving prey they favour, being long, straight and sharp. They have curved claws and use their tails for counter-balance. A special pump in their throat allows them to breathe while running, despite one lung at a time being squashed when they are in this position.

RATTLESNAKE

(Scientific name: Crotalus)

Eats: mice, rats, small birds and other small animals

6

These ambush predators are equipped with a powerful venom that spells the end for their prey.

PREDATOR POINTS

SCARY STATS: 6/10

TERRIFYING TECHNIQUES: 6/10

LETHAL WEAPONS: 8/10

PREDATOR SCORE: 20/30

SPEEDY AND POISONOUS KILLERS

LETHAL WEAPONS:

Rattlesnakes use their long, hinged fangs for injecting their venom. They are also able to decide how much to use on their prey, depending on how big it is (which is handy since it takes a while for their stores to replenish after use). Their venom usually immobilizes rather than kills.

SCARY STATS:

Rattlesnakes vary in size from 50 centimetres (19.6 in) to 2 metres (5.6 ft). They are the number one contributor to snakebite injuries in humans in North America. They can strike in half a second and during a strike their mouth can open to 180 degrees. Large rattlesnakes have fangs 10–15 centimetres (4–6 in) long.

TERRIFYING TECHNIQUES:

As ambush predators, rattlesnakes lie in wait for their prey, or hunt for it in holes. They strike it quickly with a venomous bite. If it escapes before they are able to eat it, they follow it using smell and prod it with their head to make sure it is out of action, before swallowing it whole.

BURMESE PYTHON

(Scientific name: Python bivittatus)

Eats: birds and mammals

Another kind of snake that kills by constriction, Burmese pythons are huge and frightening predators.

SCARY STATS:

One of the five biggest species of snake in the world, and with females considerably heavier and more solid than males, these pythons average 3.7 metres (12.1 ft) in length and 29 kilograms (63.9 lbs) in weight but have been known to reach a gigantic 5.74 metres (18.8 ft).

TERRIFYING TECHNIQUES:

Like boas, Burmese pythons use their teeth to grab prey and then wrap their huge bodies around it to squeeze it to death. They are excellent climbers and swimmers and can stay underwater for up to half an hour. Their whole digestive system and heart expand after eating to process the meal.

LETHAL WEAPONS:

Burmese pythons' sharp backwards-pointing teeth help them to seize prey, while their huge bulk and muscles are needed to crush it in their coils. Their massively flexible jaws enable them to engulf prey whole. These jaws also have heat sensors, which allow the snake to locate prey.

PREDATOR POINTS

SCARY STATS: 8/10
TERRIFYING TECHNIQUES: 7/10
LETHAL WEAPONS: 7/10
PREDATOR SCORE: 22/30
MASSIVE AND MUSCLY

SCARY STATS: 6/10

TERRIFYING TECHNIQUES: 8/10

LETHAL WEAPONS: 9/10

PREDATOR SCORE: 23/30

CUNNING DISGUISE COMBINED
WITH LETHAL FORCE

ALLIGATOR SNAPPING
TURTLE

(Scientific name: Macrochelys temminckii)

Eats: almost anything they can catch but mostly fish, molluscs and amphibians

4

The ridges on this turtle's shell which look like alligator skin explain the first part of its name. The second comes from the deadly clamp of its jaws once prey has been lured into its mouth.

SCARY STATS:

Males are much bigger than females, averaging lengths of 66 centimetres (26 in) and 79 kilograms (175 lbs). They are the largest freshwater turtle in North America, and among the largest in the world. Their bite is powerful enough to chop through the handle of a broom!

TERRIFYING TECHNIQUES:

These turtles typically lie motionless in the water with their mouths open. These are camouflaged to their surroundings and equipped with a worm-like appendage, so prey will swim or float straight in, in search of a tasty morsel. The turtle then snaps its mouth shut, as its name suggests.

LETHAL WEAPONS:

The bright red worm-like growth sits on tip of the turtle's tongue and acts as a lure, as it moves around like a worm. The turtles also have strong jaws and necks that can behave like springs, both of which complete the capture of prey, as well as a very forceful bite.

PUFF ADDER

(Scientific name: Bitis arietans)

Eats: mammals, birds, amphibians and lizards

Responsible for causing the most human deaths by snakebite in Africa, the puff adder is an aggressive predator that is readily angered.

PREDATOR POINTS

SCARY STATS: 7/10

TERRIFYING TECHNIQUES: 9/10

LETHAL WEAPONS: 8/10

PREDATOR SCORE: 24/30

TOXIC VENOM PLUS A FIERCE STRIKE

SCARY STATS:

Puff adders are on average 1 metre (3.3 ft) long and very stout. Especially large examples weigh over 6 kilograms (13.2 lbs) and measure 40 centimetres (16 in) in diameter. They can strike to a distance of about a third of their body length.

LETHAL WEAPONS :

These snakes are well-camouflaged, enabling them to stay hidden from their prey. Their fangs are long and sharp enough to pierce leather. They have strong venom which they produce in large amounts – enough to kill a human. This venom acts by destroying tissue and is one of the most toxic of any viper snake's.

TERRIFYING TECHNIQUES:

Puff adders are excellent climbers and have been found as high as 4.6 metres (15.1 ft) above the ground. They are also good swimmers. Usually sluggish, these ambush predators can move very quickly when agitated. The force of their bite and the depth they can pierce with their fangs means that death is often caused by physical trauma alone.

AMERICAN ALLIGATOR

(Scientific name: Alligator mississippiensis)

Eats: fish, insects, crustaceans, snails and worms

2

Apex predators in their natural habitat, alligators are a deadly combination of size, speed and strength.

SCARY STATS:

Impressively big predators, alligators reach an average length of 4 metres (13.1 ft) and a weight of 360 kilograms (793.6 lbs). Especially large males can reach 454 kilograms (1000 lbs).

TERRIFYING TECHNIQUES:

Alligators use a "death roll" to kill animals that are too big to be destroyed in one bite. This means biting prey, spinning and tearing off chunks.

LETHAL WEAPONS:

Alligators have very strong muscles for closing their jaws, though those for opening them are weaker. Their tail is important for performing the death roll.

KILLER FACT

ALLIGATORS CAN WALK A SHORT DISTANCE ON THEIR HIND LEGS AND ARE CAPABLE OF BRIEF BURSTS OF SPEED.

GREEN ANACONDA

(Scientific name: Eunectes murinus)

Eats: a wide variety of prey including fish, birds, mammals and other reptiles

Gram for gram the biggest snake in the world, green anacondas are ferocious predators, capable of eating prey as big as jaguars.

1

SCARY STATS:

These massive snakes measure up to a humungous 5.21 metres (17.1 ft) and have an average weight of 227 kilograms (500 lbs), making them the heaviest snake in the world. The "eunectes" part of their name comes from the Greek for "good swimmer" and they can reach speeds of 16 kilometres per hour (10 mph).

KILLER FACT

GREEN ANACONDAS SOMETIMES ENGAGE IN CANNIBALISM, USUALLY WITH THE LARGER FEMALES PREYING ON THE SMALLER MALES.

TERRIFYING TECHNIQUES:

Green anacondas often lie mostly submerged in water, watching and waiting for prey to come by. These non-venomous constrictors then seize the prey with their teeth and use their huge size to subdue it, before their stretchy jaw muscles open wide to swallow it whole.

LETHAL WEAPONS:

This snake's eyes and nostrils are in the top of its head, allowing it to wait with almost all of its body underwater while keeping a look-out for prey. Its body is huge and muscular, which is how it constricts its victims until powerless. Once swallowed, prey continues to be constricted within the snake's body until it is dead.

Did you know?

Anacondas' large meals can take a long time to digest, allowing them to go weeks or even months without eating again.

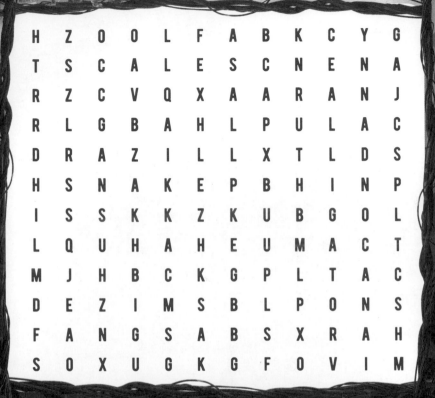

```
H Z O O L F A B K C Y G
T S C A L E S C N E N A
R Z C V Q X A A R A N J
R L G B A H L P U L A C
D R A Z I L L X T L D S
H S N A K E P B H I N P
I S S K K Z K U B G O L
L Q U H A H E U M A C T
M J H B C K G P L T A C
D E Z I M S B L P O N S
F A N G S A B S X R A H
S O X U G K G F O V I M
```

Can you find these eight words hidden in the grid above?

ALLIGATOR • AMBUSH • ANACONDA • FANGS
LIZARD • PREY • SCALES • SNAKE

TEST YOUR KNOWLEDGE!

Now that you've read all about these terrifying predators, see if you can answer these tricky questions.

1. What do Mexican beaded lizards use to smell their prey?

a. a nose on the top of their heads   b. their tongues

c. their ears

2. How long can the Asian water monitor stay underwater for?

a. 30 minutes   b. 15 minutes   c. 45 minutes

3. How does the alligator snapping turtle attract its prey?

a. by giving off a special scent

b. by dangling a worm-like appendage in its mouth

c. by making a noise

4. Which predator uses a death roll to kill its prey?

a. a Burmese python   b. a puff adder   c. an alligator

5. What do the special cells in a boa constrictor's lips do?

a. they are heat sensors   b. they help to taste food

c. they are used to smell prey

Answers on page 75

TINY TERRORS

The predators in this section might be small, but don't let that fool you. With tools such as venomous saliva, trap-building skills and mighty jaws at their disposal, these mini monsters are just as terrifying as the bigger beasts.

TIGER BEETLE

(Scientific name: Cicindelinae)

Eats: other insects

These beetles – and their larvae too – are known for their aggressive predatory style.

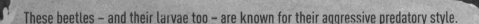

SCARY STATS:

Measuring up to 10 millimetres (0.4 in), like most of the creatures in this category tiger beetles' fearsomeness does not come from their size. They are, however, super speedy, able to move at up to 9 kilometres per hour (5.6 mph) per hour – that's the equivalent of 125 body lengths per second!

TERRIFYING TECHNIQUES:

Tiger beetles use their speed to spring forwards in pursuit of prey. Sometimes they have to stop to visually orient themselves – this is because their eyes can't always keep up with their pace! Tiger beetle larvae are also extremely predatory. They use their humpbacks to flip themselves backwards for the purpose of catching food.

LETHAL WEAPONS:

Tiger beetles are super-fast both on the ground and in the air. They have large, powerful jaws, which they use to grab their prey. Their antennae prevent them from running into things when moving fast. This reflects the fact, however, that their eyesight is not always sharp enough to keep up with their speed.

PREDATOR POINTS

SCARY STATS: 4/10

TERRIFYING TECHNIQUES: 5/10

LETHAL WEAPONS: 2/10

PREDATOR SCORE: 11/30

SUPER SPEED AND A POWERFUL BITE

NEW ZEALAND GLOWWORM

(Scientific name: Arachnocampa luminosa)

Eats: midges, mayflies, mosquitoes, moths, small snails and millipedes

These glowworm larvae may look like beautiful stars twinkling in the darkness, but they are ruthless predators.

SCARY STATS:

Larvae are a tiny 3–5 millimetres (0.12–0.19 in) long when they emerge from their eggs. However, they can produce as many as 70 threads of silk of 30–40 centimetres (11.8–15.7 in) in length, which they dangle to grab prey. They then reel these threads in at a rate of about 2 millimetres (0.07 in) per second.

TERRIFYING TECHNIQUES:

The larvae produce a glow – caused by a chemical reaction – to entice prey into the threads that they dangle, which are called "snares". A hungry larva glows more brightly than one that has just eaten. Snares hold droplets of mucus which prey sticks to. Once prey is caught, the larvae eats the snare to reel it in.

LETHAL WEAPONS:

Glowworm larvae ideally live out of the wind so their snares do not become tangled. When growing in a more exposed area the threads do not grow as long. Snares are also sensitive to light and stop glowing when touched. As well as their snares, larvae create nests for themselves out of their silk threads.

PREDATOR POINTS

SCARY STATS: 1/10

TERRIFYING TECHNIQUES: 6/10

LETHAL WEAPONS: 5/10

PREDATOR SCORE: 12/30

A NIGHT SKY THAT BITES

SCARY STATS: 3/10

TERRIFYING TECHNIQUES: 5/10

LETHAL WEAPONS: 5/10

PREDATOR SCORE: 13/30

A FORMIDABLE AND SAVAGE PREDATOR

PRAYING MANTIS

(Scientific name: Mantodea)

Eats: fruit flies, crickets, beetles, moths, bees and other insects

These are such notorious predators that people commonly mistake the spelling of their name as "*preying* mantis".

8

SCARY STATS:

Praying mantises still fit comfortably within our Tiny Terrors section, measuring on average 5–12 centimetres (1.96–4.72 in). However, they have many tools to make up for their lack of size. For example, they each have five eyes and can turn their heads 180 degrees. They can complete jumps in a tenth of a second.

TERRIFYING TECHNIQUES:

The majority of praying mantises are ambush predators that prefer to eat their victims while they're still alive! They employ their elaborate camouflage to stalk or lie in wait for prey, and their hunting relies heavily on their excellent vision. Once they have located their prey, mantises seize it with their forelegs.

LETHAL WEAPONS:

Praying mantises' forelegs are spiked, making them the perfect weapon for grabbing their victims. Their incredible eyesight can be described as "stereo" – meaning they can see in 3D. In some species, the mantis's gut can extend to the whole length of its body, allowing it to store prey for later digestion.

PREDATOR POINTS

SCARY STATS: 2/10

TERRIFYING TECHNIQUES: 6/10

LETHAL WEAPONS: 6/10

PREDATOR SCORE: 14/30

GRASPING LEGS AND A PAINFUL BITE

WATER SCORPION

(Scientific name: Nepidae)

Eats: small insects such as water fleas and water worms

These ambush predators are not like true land scorpions – but they take their name from the grasping forelegs that they have in common with them.

7

SCARY STATS:

These diminutive predators measure 25–52 millimetres (0.98–2.04 in) in length. They can stay underwater for up to 30 minutes, using their tail as a kind of snorkel.

TERRIFYING TECHNIQUES:

When underwater, these predators stay completely still, waiting for prey to pass by. When it does, they ambush it, seizing it with their hook-like legs.

KILLER FACT

WATER SCORPIONS ARE SOMETIMES USED FOR PEST CONTROL.

LETHAL WEAPONS:

In addition to their deadly legs that they use like pincers, and their tails that are employed for breathing underwater, these aquatic hunters have sucking mouthparts. Their eggs have long hairs, which supply them with oxygen. Adult water scorpions are not strong swimmers; they move around mostly by walking.

PORTIA SPIDER

(Scientific name: Portia)

Eats: web-building spiders up to 200 times its own size

Portia spiders are notorious for their highly intelligent hunting behaviour, which they can adapt according to the prey, and can learn from by trial and error.

LETHAL WEAPONS:

Portia spiders have complex eyes that allow them to see at a significant distance and in great detail, even if focusing can take them some time. They sometimes use their silk threads as abseiling wires to drop down on prey from behind. However their greatest weapon is probably their intelligence.

PREDATOR POINTS

SCARY STATS: 2/10

TERRIFYING TECHNIQUES: 8/10

LETHAL WEAPONS: 5/10

PREDATOR SCORE: 15/30

MEGA-INTELLIGENT HUNTERS

SCARY STATS:

Portia spiders are truly tiny, measuring only 5–10 millimetres (0.19–0.39 in), but their predatory prowess is considerable nonetheless. They can see objects up to about 75 centimetres (29.5 in) away, though it does take them a while to focus. They can jump up to 15 times their own height.

TERRIFYING TECHNIQUES:

When hunting, these spiders demonstrate terrifying intelligence, adapting their technique depending on the prey they've set their sights on. They even trial new techniques, and reuse them if successful. They make detours to ensure the best direction of attack, can imitate the vibrations of trapped prey to act as bait for other spiders; and can camouflage themselves as leaves.

ASSASSIN BUG

(Scientific name: Reduviidae)

Eats: other insects, mammal blood

5

Assassin bugs are aptly named, with their especially gruesome method of killing their victims. They are sometimes nicknamed the "kissing bug" as they're known to bite humans around the lips!

PREDATOR POINTS

SCARY STATS: 2/10

TERRIFYING TECHNIQUES: 6/10

LETHAL WEAPONS: 8/10

PREDATOR SCORE: 16/30

STAB AND SLURP

SCARY STATS:

There are about 7000 species of assassin bug measuring between 4–40 millimetres (0.15–1.57 in) in length, although on average they are at the larger end of this scale. One species can project its deadly venom as far as 30 centimetres (12 in).

TERRIFYING TECHNIQUES:

Assassin bugs are truly sneaky predators – they use the noise of the wind blowing to cover the sound of their approach, and their unusual way of moving means that they don't cause vibrations when creeping across spider webs. They stalk or lure prey before stabbing it with their sharp, curved mouthparts.

LETHAL WEAPONS:

Assassin bugs inject venomous saliva into their prey through their mouthparts. The prey's innard are liquefied by the venom and can then be sucked up through the mouthparts as though through a straw! This saliva is strong enough to kill prey much bigger than the bug itself.

SCARY STATS: 2/10

TERRIFYING TECHNIQUES: 6/10

LETHAL WEAPONS: 9/10

PREDATOR SCORE: 17/30

DEATH JAWS

SAFARI ANTS

(Scientific name: Dorylus)

Eats: spiders, small mammals

4

These ferocious ants are notorious for their powerful jaws, so strong that they have been known to be used as emergency stitches for humans!

SCARY STATS:

Safari ants range in size from tiny worker ants measuring 5 millimetres (0.19 in) to the queen who can grow up to 5 centimetres (1.96 in). They move in columns of up to 50,000,000 to look for food when it becomes scarce – though they don't move very fast, covering only 20 metres (65.6 ft) every hour!

TERRIFYING TECHNIQUES:

These ants are capable of stinging, but more often use their deadly jaws. Large numbers of them can overwhelm small animals to kill or immobilize them, before eating their flesh.

LETHAL WEAPONS:

Safari ants rely on their huge numbers and on their strong and sharp jaws to subdue and destroy their victims.

KILLER FACT

IF A SAFARI ANT BITES YOU, THEIR POWERFUL JAWS CLAMP SO TIGHTLY SHUT THAT YOU CAN PULL THE ANT'S BODY IN TWO BEFORE MANAGING TO REMOVE THEM!

SCARY STATS: 5/10

TERRIFYING TECHNIQUES: 5/10

LETHAL WEAPONS: 8/10

PREDATOR SCORE: 18/30

WORLD'S MOST VENOMOUS SPIDER

BRAZILIAN WANDERING SPIDER

(Scientific name: Phoneutria)

Eats: crickets and other large insects, small lizards, mice

While these spiders have no interest in eating humans, they are dangerous when disturbed, and possess a nasty venom.

3

SCARY STATS:

This predator has the questionable honour of being the world's most venomous spider. Typical body lengths are 17–48 millimetres (0.67–1.89 in) and leg lengths are 13–15 centimetres (5.1–5.9 in).

TERRIFYING TECHNIQUES:

Nocturnal hunters, these spiders wander the forest floor, actively seeking prey, rather than building webs. They use their highly toxic venom to immobilize prey.

KILLER FACT

THESE SPIDERS LIKE TO HIDE IN DARK PLACES – SUCH AS HOUSES, CARS OR SHOES!

LETHAL WEAPONS:

As well as being extremely potent, Brazilian wandering spiders' toxic venom is incredibly painful for the victim. Without treatment, the venom can even cause death in humans. However, it is estimated that the spiders only deliver venom in a third of their bites.

ROBBER FLY

(Scientific name: Asilidae)

Eats: other insects

These sturdy flies are infamously aggressive predators who possess a grisly range of weapons and techniques to turn the most robust tummy!

LETHAL WEAPONS:

The robber fly's savage, short and sharp proboscis (mouthpart) is its main weapon, used for both stabbing its victims and then sucking up their liquefied insides. The fly's saliva contains enzymes (proteins) that quickly paralyse prey and begin to digest it. These flies also possess a bristly moustache which protects them from struggling prey.

TERRIFYING TECHNIQUES:

These predators are excellent flyers, able to catch their prey in the air. They have also been observed positioning themselves at strategic points in order to ambush their targets. Prey is immobilized by a stab from their vicious mouthparts, which inject saliva that turns the victims to liquid.

SCARY STATS:

Robber flies have an average body length of 1–1.5 centimetres (0.39–0.59 in), although especially large examples grow as big as 5 centimetres (1.96 in). There are over 7000 species of robber fly and they can be found all over the world.

PREDATOR POINTS

SCARY STATS: 3/10

TERRIFYING TECHNIQUES: 8/10

LETHAL WEAPONS: 8/10

PREDATOR SCORE: 19/30

STABBING FLIES

ANTLION

(*Scientific name: Myrmeleontidae*)

Eats: insects, especially ants

(1)

It is the larvae of this species rather than the fully-grown antlion that is the most brutal predator in this section.

Did you know?

Adult antlions don't eat, so it's up to the larva to consume enough to sustain the adult throughout the rest of its life.

TERRIFYING TECHNIQUES:

To catch prey, antlion larvae dig pits into the sand, then lie in wait at the bottom. When a victim slips into the trap, the antlion snaps it up with its killer jaws. Any attempt to escape is thwarted by the larva showering prey with loose sand or soil. Larvae are highly sensitive to the vibrations in the ground caused by approaching victims.

KILLER FACT

ONCE THEY'VE DRAINED VICTIMS OF ALL THEIR FLUIDS, ANTLION LARVAE FLICK THEIR VICTIMS' DRY BODIES OUT OF THEIR TRAPS TO DISCARD THEM.

SCARY STATS:

Larvae measure only about 1.5 centimetres (0.59 in), but the pits or traps which many species dig for their prey are about 5 centimetres (1.96 in) deep and 7.5 centimetres (2.95 in) wide. Adult antlions have wingspans ranging from 2–15 centimetres (0.78–5.9 in).

LETHAL WEAPONS:

Larvae have sharp, pincer-like jaws which have hollow parts that allow them to inject venom and then suck out the juices from the prey. They are covered in bristles which enable them to root their bodies firmly and therefore overpower prey much bigger than themselves.

PREDATOR POINTS

SCARY STATS: 5/10

TERRIFYING TECHNIQUES: 9/10

LETHAL WEAPONS: 9/10

PREDATOR SCORE: 23/30

TERRIFYING TRAP-BUILDERS

TRUE OR FALSE?

Can you say whether the statements below are true or false?

	TRUE	FALSE
1. Tiger beetle larvae flip themselves backwards to catch prey.		
2. A praying mantis can turn its head 360 degrees.		
3. Water scorpions use their tails as a snorkel.		
4. Portia spiders use their silk threads to weave webs.		
5. The assassin bug dissolves its victim's insides with venom.		
6. The Brazilian wandering spider catches its prey in webs.		
7. The robber fly's main weapon is its proboscis.		
8. A fully-grown antlion doesn't eat anything.		

MINI MONSTER MATCH

Can you draw a line to match
the tiny terror to its picture?

A. PRAYING MANTIS •

B. BRAZILIAN WANDERING SPIDER •

C. PORTIA SPIDER •

D. ROBBER FLY •

E. TIGER BEETLE •

F. WATER SCORPION •

Answers on page 75

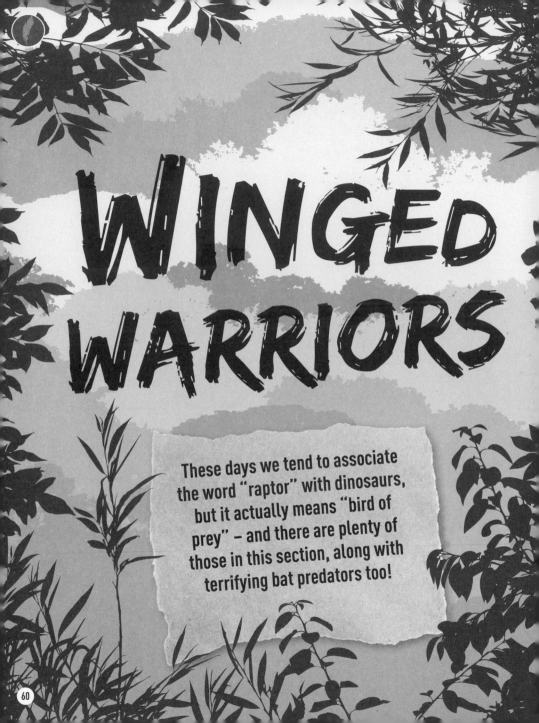

WINGED WARRIORS

These days we tend to associate the word "raptor" with dinosaurs, but it actually means "bird of prey" – and there are plenty of those in this section, along with terrifying bat predators too!

BUZZARD

(Scientific name: Buteo buteo)

Eats: small rodents, reptiles, amphibians, larger insects and earthworms and other birds

SCARY STATS: 7/10
TERRIFYING TECHNIQUES: 5/10
LETHAL WEAPONS: 5/10
PREDATOR SCORE: 17/30
GLIDING HUNTERS

These wide-ranging raptors can often be seen hanging in the air ready to drop down on unsuspecting prey.

SCARY STATS:

Measuring 40–58 centimetres in length (16–23 in), with wingspans of 104–109 centimetres (43–55 in) and weights of 427 grams to 1.4 kilograms (0.94–3 lbs) – females being larger than males – buzzards are medium-sized birds of prey, and the most common and widespread in the UK.

LETHAL WEAPONS:

Buzzards use their broad wings – sometimes held in a V shape – to soar and glide or hang in the air while keeping watch for likely-looking meals. However, they are slow flyers and usually complete their kills on the ground where their mighty talons are employed to grab their prey.

TERRIFYING TECHNIQUES:

Buzzards are fiercely territorial and prefer to hunt over open land. They either wait and watch for prey from a perch, before flying in for the attack once it is located, or glide and hang in the wind before dropping down on their victims, or simply walk across the ground in pursuit.

PHILIPPINE EAGLE

(Scientific name: Pithecophaga jefferyi)

Eats: bats, birds and small to medium-sized mammals (including monkeys!)

9

These birds are apex predators in their habitat, and are large, swift and nimble hunters.

PREDATOR POINTS

SCARY STATS: 6/10

TERRIFYING TECHNIQUES: 6/10

LETHAL WEAPONS: 6/10

PREDATOR SCORE: 18/30

CRITICALLY ENDANGERED
BUT RUTHLESS RAPTORS

SCARY STATS:

Philippine eagles range in size from 80–102 centimetres (31–40 in), with tails of 42–45 centimetres (16.5–18 in) and wingspans up to a massive 1.8 metres (6 ft). They weigh 4.7–8 kilograms (10.3–17.6 lbs). These opportunistic predators take prey ranging from 10 grams (0.02 lbs), such as a small bat, to 14 kilograms (30.8 lbs), such as a deer.

TERRIFYING TECHNIQUES:

These eagles are very fast and agile flyers. They use both still-hunting – meaning they sit almost motionless in trees to watch for prey – and perch-hunting, which involves moving from resting place to resting place, often in a downwards direction. Young Philippine eagles have been spotted attacking inanimate objects for hunting practice.

LETHAL WEAPONS:

Philippine eagles have large, powerful legs, and claws which can grow up to 13 centimetres (5.1 in) for snatching their victims, as well as impressive hooked beaks – among the biggest of any eagle – for tearing them apart. They also have excellent eyesight – they're able to see eight times the distance a human can.

SPECTRAL BAT

(Scientific name: Vampyrum spectrum)

Eats: small birds and mammals, amphibians and reptiles

PREDATOR POINTS

SCARY STATS: 6/10

TERRIFYING TECHNIQUES: 6/10

LETHAL WEAPONS: 8/10

PREDATOR SCORE: 20/30

WINGED MEAT-EATERS

While the majority of the world's bat species feed on insects, fruit or nectar, these predators eat meat.

SCARY STATS:

The largest carnivorous bat in the world, these hunters measure 12.5–13.5 centimetres (4.9–5.3 in) in length, with wingspans of 60–91.5 centimetres (23.6–36 in), and weigh 145–190 grams (319.6–418.8 lbs).

TERRIFYING TECHNIQUES:

These stealthy predators are very agile in flight. When hunting, they fly slowly and low to the ground, and use all their senses including echolocation.

LETHAL WEAPONS:

Spectral bats have a wing structure that allows them to carry heavy prey and to move in tight spaces. Their sense of smell is their most useful tool in hunting for prey.

KILLER FACT

SPECTRAL BATS WERE ORIGINALLY CONFUSED WITH VAMPIRE BATS, WHICH FEED ON THE BLOOD OF LARGER ANIMALS, USUALLY WITHOUT NEEDING TO KILL THEM.

PREDATOR POINTS

SCARY STATS: 7/10

TERRIFYING TECHNIQUES: 6/10

LETHAL WEAPONS: 8/10

PREDATOR SCORE: 21/30

LITERALLY HAWK-EYED HUNTERS

HAWK

(Scientific name: Accipitridae)

Eats: snakes, lizards, fish, birds, mice, rabbits, squirrels and other small animals

The name "hawk" covers a wide range of subspecies but all birds in this family use their keen eyesight in pursuit of their prey.

SCARY STATS:

Measuring 45–65 centimetres (17.7–25.6 in) with wingspans of 58–68 centimetres (22.8–26.7 in), and weighing 630 grams to 1.4 kilograms (1.38–3.08 lbs), these are medium-sized birds of prey.

TERRIFYING TECHNIQUES:

Hawks usually hunt by making a sudden dash from a hiding place, and kill their prey using their claws.

KILLER FACT

THE FATTER A HAWK IS WHEN IT BEGINS ITS ANNUAL MIGRATION, THE MORE LIKELY IT IS TO COMPLETE THE TRIP SAFELY.

LETHAL WEAPONS:

Hawks are famously sharp-sighted. Their eyes have four kinds of colour receptors and a large number of light receptors. Nerves connect these receptors to the brain, allowing these birds to see the ultraviolet part of the spectrum, as well as to detect magnetic fields. They are also highly intelligent birds.

OSPREY

(Scientific name: Pandion haliaetus)

Eats: fish

6

These birds of prey live close to the water and have developed the perfect hunting techniques and tools for their habitat.

LETHAL WEAPONS:

Ospreys have reversible outer toes – being able to grab prey with two toes in front and two behind is very handy when hunting slippery fish. Their vision is well-adapted to locating prey underwater and from a great height. Their nostrils can close to keep out water during dives.

PREDATOR POINTS

SCARY STATS: 7/10

TERRIFYING TECHNIQUES: 8/10

LETHAL WEAPONS: 7/10

PREDATOR SCORE: 22/30

PIRATE PREDATORS

SCARY STATS:

These birds are usually more than 60 centimetres (23.6 in) in length with 180 centimetre (70.8 in) wingspans, and they weigh 900 grams to 2.1 kilograms (1.98–4.62 lbs). They like their food on the large side, typically taking fish weighing 150–300 grams (0.33–0.66 lbs).

TERRIFYING TECHNIQUES:

Ospreys hover, soar and glide above water, using their excellent eyesight to look for prey. Once it is located, they plunge towards the water feet first – they are able to go as deep as 91 centimetres (3ft) – and seize the prey with their talons.

SCARY STATS: 6/10

TERRIFYING TECHNIQUES: 8/10

LETHAL WEAPONS: 9/10

PREDATOR SCORE: 23/30

NOCTURNAL TERRORS

GREAT HORNED OWL

5

(Scientific name: Strigiformes)

Eats: insects and small rodents

Great horned owls use their amazing night-time vision and their super-strong legs and talons to find and kill their victims.

SCARY STATS:

The heaviest owl in South and Central America, with females slightly larger than males, these birds have an average weight of 1.4 kilograms (3.12 lbs) and a wingspan of 91–153 centimetres (3–5 ft).

TERRIFYING TECHNIQUES:

Great horned owls fly from perch to perch looking for prey before swooping down to ambush it. They can fly at speeds of more than 65 kilometres per hour (40 mph).

LETHAL WEAPONS:

These owls have incredibly strong feet and sharp talons that they use to crush and stab their prey. Their beaks are also sometimes used for biting and tearing. Their colouring helps them to camouflage into their surroundings. They have very big eyes – even by the standards of other owls – which help with their nocturnal vision.

KILLER FACT

GREAT HORNED OWLS CAN TURN THEIR NECKS 270 DEGREES.

BEARDED VULTURE

(Scientific name: Gypaetus barbatus)

Eats: bones of a wide range of creatures; tortoises

The bearded vulture has a diet consisting almost entirely of bone. They often tear through the flesh of the prey without eating it to get to the skeleton!

LETHAL WEAPONS:

Bearded vultures' stomach acid is adapted to be able to digest bone. They attack live prey more regularly than any other kind of vulture, using their huge and powerful wings to sweep large victims to their deaths. They are strong enough to be able to carry prey their own weight.

TERRIFYING TECHNIQUES:

These birds can swallow or bite through bones up to the size of a lamb's thigh bone. Bones bigger than this are carried to a great height and then dropped to crack them open. Larger animals are killed by being battered by the vultures' wings and pushed off sheer drops.

SCARY STATS:

Bearded vultures typically measure 94–125 centimetres (3–4.1 ft), with massive wingspans of 2.31–2.83 metres (7.6–9.3 ft), and weigh 4.8–7.5 kilograms (10.5–16.5 lbs). Females are slightly larger than males. Their diet is 85–90% bone marrow and they are able to digest large bones in 24 hours.

PREDATOR POINTS

SCARY STATS: 8/10

TERRIFYING TECHNIQUES: 9/10

LETHAL WEAPONS: 7/10

PREDATOR SCORE: 24/30

TERRIFYING BONE-CRUNCHERS

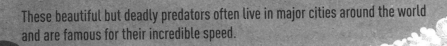

PEREGRINE FALCON

(Scientific name: Falco peregrinus)

Eats: medium-sized birds such as pigeons and doves

These beautiful but deadly predators often live in major cities around the world and are famous for their incredible speed.

SCARY STATS:

Peregrine falcons' most impressive statistic is that they can reach speeds of 320 kilometres per hour (198.8 mph) on one of their legendary dives – this makes them the world's fastest member of the animal kingdom! Their body length is 34–58 centimetres (13.3–22.8 in) with wingspans of 74–120 centimetres (29.1–47.2 in).

TERRIFYING TECHNIQUES:

Peregrine falcons were traditionally used by humans for hunting. They swoop down on prey at an almost unbelievable speed in their hunting dive, usually capturing it in mid-air and striking it with a clenched foot that either stuns or kills it. They also kill prey by snapping its spine with their beak.

LETHAL WEAPONS:

Peregrine falcons' eyes and nostrils are adapted to allow for the pressure of their super-swift dives. Their upper beak is notched in such a way that they can cut through the spine of their prey, and their feet are strong enough to kill their victims through impact alone.

PREDATOR POINTS

SCARY STATS: 9/10

TERRIFYING TECHNIQUES: 8/10

LETHAL WEAPONS: 8/10

PREDATOR SCORE: 25/30

WORLD'S FASTEST ANIMAL

HARPY EAGLE

(Scientific name: Harpia harpyja)

Eats: tree-dwelling mammals

2

These apex predators are the most powerful birds of prey in the rainforest, with talons that are amongst the longest in the animal kingdom.

SCARY STATS:

Harpy eagles have huge talons of 7.6–10.1 centimetres (3–4 in). Females are the larger of the species, measuring 86.5–107 centimetres (34–42 in) in length, with wingspans of 176–224 centimetres (69.2–88.1 in), and weighing 6–9 kilograms (13.2–19.8 lbs). They regularly take prey weighing more than 7 kilograms (15.4 lbs).

TERRIFYING TECHNIQUES:

These predators sometimes sit and wait for prey to pass by, but more often move from perch to perch in search of it or pursue it through the trees. When dealing with prey heavier than themselves they either eat it at the site of killing or tear it into pieces to carry back to their nest.

LETHAL WEAPONS:

As well as their enormous talons, which are the same length as a grizzly bear's, and their incredibly powerful grip, those birds have legs almost the width of a human wrist, which helps them to carry heavy prey. Their long tails assist them in steering through thick vegetation.

BALD EAGLE

(Scientific name: Haliaeetus leucocephalus)   Eats: fish, birds and mammals

These apex predators in their habitat are both strong and swift, and are the national animal of the USA.

SCARY STATS:

Bald eagles are powerful flyers, able to reach speeds of 56–70 kilometres per hour (34.7–43.4 mph) and dive speeds of 120–160 kilometres per hour (74.5–99.1 mph). Their gripping strength is calculated to be ten times that of a human. They measure 70–102 centimetres (27.5–40.1 in) with wingspans of 1.8–2.3 metres (5.9–7.5 ft).

PREDATOR POINTS

SCARY STATS: 9/10
TERRIFYING TECHNIQUES: 9/10
LETHAL WEAPONS: 9/10
PREDATOR SCORE: 27/30

GIANT AND SKILFUL HUNTERS

KILLER FACT

BALD EAGLES ARE CAPABLE OF KILLING OFF THE MAJORITY OF A SEABIRD COLONY.

LETHAL WEAPONS:

Bald eagles have highly developed hind toes that they use to pierce vital areas of their victims while they are held still by the large front talons. Their toes are also well-adapted to holding slippery fish. They have big, hooked beaks and can store food in a pouch in their throat.

Did you know?

Bald eagles aren't actually bald. Their name comes from an old definition of the word "piebald" meaning "white headed".

TERRIFYING TECHNIQUES:

These ferocious hunters are fast and highly manoeuvrable in flight, and have been known to fly underneath prey to sink their talons into its exposed underbelly. They often swoop down to snatch fish from the water with their talons too. They sometimes steal prey away from other predators.

Can you fit these words into the spaces?
The first two have been done for you.

HUNT   RAPTOR

~~NEST~~   SPEED

POWERFUL   TALONS

~~PREDATOR~~ WINGSPAN

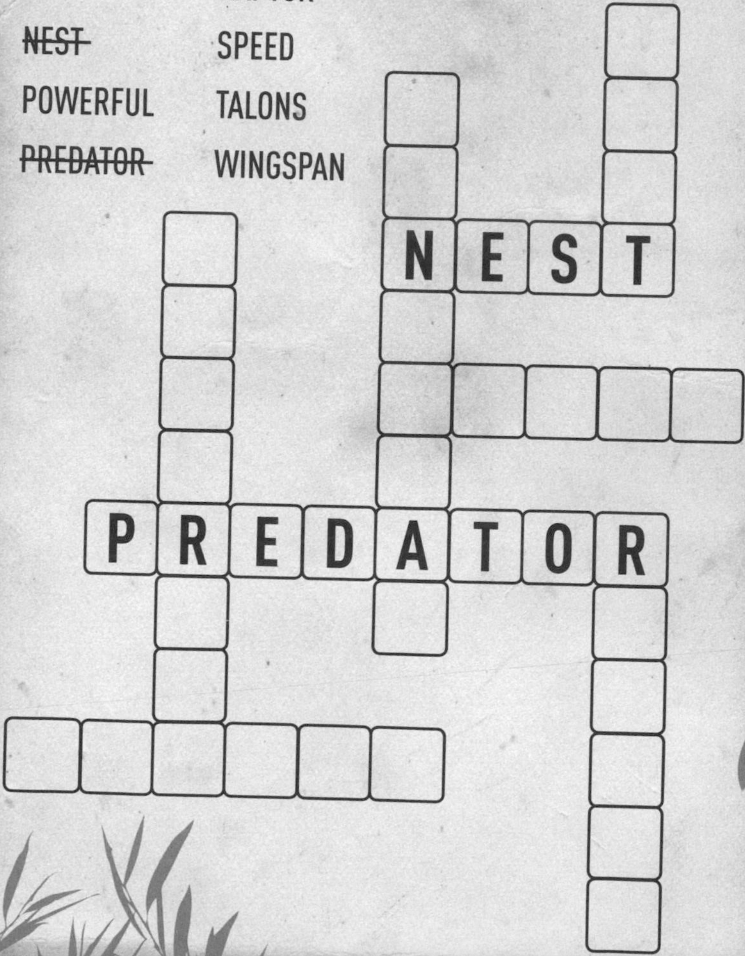

N E S T

P R E D A T O R

FLY MAZE

Can you guide the bald eagle fly through the maze to grab the fish?

Answers on page 76

ACTIVITY ANSWERS

PAGES 16–17

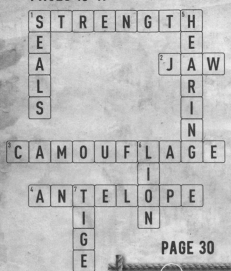

```
¹S T R E N G T ⁵H
E           H
A         ²J A W
L           A
S           R
            I
            N
³C A M O U F ⁶L A G E
            I
⁴A N⁷T E L O P E
     I      O
     G      N
     E
     R
```

PAGE 31

1. FALSE – they are 95% water!
2. TRUE
3. FALSE – they use them to slash and injure fish
4. TRUE
5. TRUE
6. FALSE – they love them!
7. TRUE
8. FALSE – they have light organs on their eyeballs that help them to see in the dark

PAGE 30

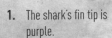

1. The shark's fin tip is purple.
2. The shark's gills have gone.
3. The bubbles above the squid have gone.
4. The squid's eyes are missing.
5. One of the fish in the corner have gone.
6. The orca has a green marking.
7. The sea grass behind the orca has gone.
8. There is now a starfish in the bottom left corner.

ACTIVITY ANSWERS

PAGE 44

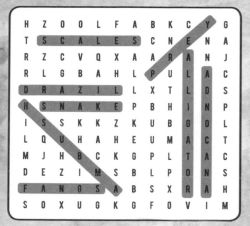

H	Z	O	O	L	F	A	B	K	C	Y	G
T	S	C	A	L	E	S	C	N	E	N	A
R	Z	C	V	Q	X	A	A	R	A	N	J
R	L	G	B	A	H	L	P	U	L	A	C
D	R	A	Z	I	L	L	X	T	L	D	S
H	S	N	A	K	E	P	B	H	I	N	P
I	S	S	K	K	Z	K	U	B	G	O	L
L	Q	U	H	A	H	E	U	M	A	C	T
M	J	H	B	C	K	G	P	L	T	A	C
D	E	Z	I	M	S	B	L	P	O	N	S
F	A	N	G	S	A	B	S	X	R	A	H
S	O	X	U	G	K	G	F	O	V	I	M

PAGE 45

1. b

2. a

3. b

4. c

5. a

PAGE 58

1. TRUE
2. FALSE – it can turn its head 180 degrees
3. TRUE
4. FALSE – they use them to catch prey
5. TRUE
6. FALSE – they don't build webs
7. TRUE
8. TRUE

PAGE 59

A. PRAYING MANTIS

B. BRAZILIAN WANDERING SPIDER

C. PORTIA SPIDER

D. ROBBER FLY

E. TIGER BEETLE

F. WATER SCORPION

ACTIVITY ANSWERS

PAGE 72

```
          H
      W   U
      I N E S T
  P   N   T
  O   G
P R E D A T O R
  E   P       A
R F U L       P
  U   A       T
T A L O N S   O
                R
```

Crossword answers:
- HUNT
- WINGSPAN
- NEST
- SPEED
- POWERFUL
- PREDATOR
- RAPTOR
- TALONS

PAGE 73